Original title:
The Window Lush

Copyright © 2025 Creative Arts Management OÜ
All rights reserved.

Author: Oliver Bennett
ISBN HARDBACK: 978-1-80581-860-1
ISBN PAPERBACK: 978-1-80581-387-3
ISBN EBOOK: 978-1-80581-860-1

Encounters with the Wild Beyond

A squirrel in a suit comes by,
He tips his hat and says, oh my!
With pockets full of acorn treats,
He offers snacks that look like meats.

A cat in boots starts to prance,
It dances lightly, what a chance!
With whiskers twitching, tail held high,
He winks and laughs as birds fly by.

A raccoon throws a grand soirée,
With masks and hats, they dance away.
He hands me cheese, and I must share,
As everyone dances without a care.

The moon peeks in, and stars align,
While critters sip on berry wine.
They toast to life, with giggles bright,
In this wild world, there's pure delight.

Explorations Through Glassy Passages

Through panes of glass, a world unfolds,
With jumpy frogs and stories untold.
A ladybug's comedy sets the stage,
As it claims the sun, like a proud old sage.

A parakeet recites a sonnet so sweet,
About his lost sock, and dancing feet.
He hops and flutters, with feathers that shine,
While squirrels bust moves, all looking divine.

I spot a gopher, quite sneaky and sly,
Stealing my chips—oh my, oh my!
He chuckles and runs, a true little thief,
Leaving me gasping in comic disbelief.

A hedgehog rolls in, all prickles and fun,
Turning the party into a pun.
With laughter that echoes through the night,
These glassy passages spark pure delight.

Glimmers of Verdant Light

In the corner, a plant so bright,
It chips away at my sleepy sight.
Leaves dance like they're throwing a ball,
While I'm just stuck here, trying not to fall.

The sun pranks me with its shining beam,
Making each leaf a rebellious dream.
I wonder if they have a party inside,
While I sip tea with no flowery pride.

Through Framed Green Dreams

Peeking through glass, what do I see?
A neighborhood squirrel as spry as can be.
He glances at me, then leaps with glee,
As if saying, 'This show's just for thee!'

I munch on snacks as the leaves sway,
Imagining nutty dialogues at play.
Do they gossip about the weather's flair?
Or share juicy tales, like who got a hair?

Nature's Gaze on Quiet Glass

The daisies drop by, all dressed in white,
Waving their heads, it's quite the sight.
A ladybug jigs like it knows a song,
While I contemplate where I belong.

The breeze rolls past with a cheeky grin,
As if to say, 'Let the fun begin!'
I laugh at their antics, oh what a show,
Nature's the star, stealing my flow.

A Portal to Blooming Whispers

A butterfly winks, what a sneaky tease,
Fluttering by with such breezy ease.
It knows my houseplant's got more flair,
Than any of my socks, I'm in despair!

The flowers chuckle in the morning light,
Plant gossip spreads, oh what a sight!
I sip my coffee, lost in their jokes,
While plotting revenge on crafty old folks.

Songs of Green in Quiet Corners

In corners where the daisies play,
A snail named Fred moves slow all day.
He sings a tune that makes them dance,
    While ants join in a tiny trance.

The grass giggles, tickling toes,
As butterflies strike silly poses.
A ladybug winks, oh what a sight,
In this wild green delight at night.

Hues of Springtime Thru the Opening

A window cracked against the breeze,
Invites the pollen, swells the trees.
A robin chirps a comical song,
While squirrels prance around all day long.

With petals flung in playful fights,
The tulips blush at silly sights.
A flower sneezes, oh so loud,
As bees parade, so proud, so proud!

Arcadia Beyond the Barriers

Past the fence where hedgehogs roam,
A party starts in nature's home.
Frogs lip-sync to a croaky tune,
While turtles dance beneath the moon.

The hedges hum a jazzy beat,
As rabbits show off fancy feet.
A picnic lunch of leaves and dew,
With all the friends in splendid view.

The Color Symphony Outside

Outside the world's a vibrant show,
Where colors clash and mingle so.
A patchwork quilt of silly glee,
With every hue, a new decree.

The clouds wear hats; they're all askew,
As rainbows peek and giggle too.
A fuss of colors spins about,
In joy and laughter, there's no doubt!

A View of Flourishing Secrets

In a garden where gnomes like to dance,
Rabbits wear hats and squirrels take a chance.
Flowers gossip in colors so bright,
While bees hum a tune, oh what a sight!

A turtle in shades takes the sun with grace,
A sunflower winks at the passing face.
With bugs in tuxedos, they put on a show,
As the vines sway to tunes we don't quite know.

Raindrops wear boots and puddles have fun,
Splishing and splashing, they race in the sun.
Each leaf a whisper, a secret divine,
In this circus of nature, where all things align.

The Border Between Two Worlds

Where shadows play games with twinkling light,
Mice jive on rooftops, what a strange sight!
A cat in a bow tie critiques the scene,
While birds argue loudly on what to preen.

The fence is an artist, all colors collide,
As kids laugh and splash in the puddles wide.
A hedgehog in glasses reads stories aloud,
To snails with their flip-flops, part of the crowd.

Tea parties held where the fence meets the sky,
Cakes made of mushrooms, oh my, oh my!
With flavors of dreams in each whimsical bite,
This border of wonders is pure sheer delight.

Soft Tapestry of Light and Leaf

Sunbeams weave tales in a quilt of green,
As critters in costumes put on a scene.
A butterfly poses, a diva so grand,
While the ants form a line, they dance hand in hand.

Gentle winds giggle, they rustle the hair,
Of daisies adorned with a sweet, sunny flair.
The laughter of branches tickles the air,
As nature spins jokes that are handed with care.

Frogs croak a tune from a mossy old log,
While shadows all waltz with a bright dancing fog.
A tapestry woven from laughter and cheer,
Makes every glance through the leaves crystal clear.

Secrets Unfolded by the Glass

In a nook by the window, the secrets abound,
With mice on a mission, and fun to be found.
A parrot named Polly recites all the gossip,
While a roguish old magpie tries to swap a lollipop.

The sun takes confessions from flowers so bold,
While tales of the raindrops are endlessly told.
With stories of puddles and fanciful beams,
What chaos and laughter, a world of bright dreams!

Each glimmer a glimpse of the fun yet to come,
As shadows compose their own rhythm, a drum.
A carnival blooms with the dawn in its grasp,
And secrets unravel, with fun in each gasp.

Rhapsody of Green Laughter

In the garden where giggles grow,
Every leaf tickles, don't you know?
The daisies dance with silly grace,
While butterflies giggle, stuck in place.

A squirrel in boots hops on a stone,
Telling jokes to the garden gnome.
The wind whispers secrets of mirth,
In this patch of joyful earth.

Sunflowers read, with quite the flair,
Puns that make the daisies stare.
Grasshoppers sing in off-key tunes,
Making friends with the laughing moons.

So come join the fun in this greenscape bright,
Where laughter echoes with sheer delight!
Plant a smile, watch it grow wide,
In this place where giggles reside.

Timeless Raindrops on Petal Ephemera

Raindrops tumble, splash, and play,
Onto petals, a merry ballet.
With each drop, a laugh takes flight,
A symphony of silly delight.

Clouds roll in with a comic frown,
Dousing flowers with a soft crown.
The rhododendrons wear tiny hats,
While daisies go splat with silly spats.

Crickets join in, tapping softly,
Dancing as they croon quite frothy.
The roses shake, drop their frowns,
In puddles, they splash, turning upside downs.

So let this rain, with humor, bind,
Nature's giggles intertwined.
Petals giggle, droplets gleam,
In a world that feels like a dream.

Nature's Palette on a Silent Canvas

On a canvas of leaves, colors collide,
Where laughter blooms and worries slide.
Amongst the hues of orange and blue,
Squirrels scribble tales anew.

Chirping birds wear rainbow hats,
Hosting parties with silly chats.
Each flower plots a prank so grand,
While bees buzz rhymes across the land.

The sun spills laughter, a radiant gold,
As trees tell tales, both bright and bold.
A butterfly flutters, a jester in flight,
Painting giggles with sheer delight.

Join the mischief in this vibrant spree,
Where nature's canvas invites you to be.
With every brushstroke, a chuckle flows,
In this realm where pure joy grows.

The Allure of Untamed Flora

In thickets wild, where humor sprouts,
Laughter lingers, without doubts.
Dandelions grinning, lost in play,
Telling tales of a sunny day.

Cacti join in, with prickly puns,
Sending giggles under the sun.
Wildflowers wink, with colors so vivid,
In this riot, joy is livid.

A porcupine donned in a sunflower crown,
Spins stories that turn frowns upside down.
Though untamed, this place sings forth,
The comedy of nature, a constant mirth.

So step into this floral spree,
Let joy grow like the tallest tree.
Amongst the wild, laughter does thrive,
In this playground, we come alive.

Nature's Palette on a Framed Horizon

Colors dance on the sill,
Sunshine jumps like a thrill,
Birds chatter, a funny crew,
Painting skies in vibrant hue.

Flowers peep with a wink,
Grass grows just to tease and link,
A butterfly wearing socks,
Tiptoeing on flower clocks.

Silly clouds float by,
Like marshmallows in the sky,
They giggle as they pass,
Whispering tales of sass.

Soaked in laughter, joy, and cheer,
Nature's canvas draws us near,
Every stroke a playful jest,
In this frame, we're truly blessed.

Serenity in a Leafy Frame

Leaves are laughing, oh so bright,
They swish and sway, a funny sight,
Giggling squirrels dart and tease,
In a game of hide and seize.

Sunlight filters, plays around,
Tickling shadows on the ground,
A snail wearing a tiny hat,
Shuffles slow, and that is that!

The breeze plays a funny tune,
Tickling flowers, oh so June,
Petals blush with every gust,
In this frame, we laugh, we trust.

Nature whispers, "Join the fun!"
As bees buzz and flowers run,
In this leafy, lively space,
Joy leaps forth—a smiling face!

A Mosaic of Green and Glass

A patchwork quilt beneath the sun,
Every patch a pun, a run,
Dandelions dance in a swirl,
Twisting, twirling, in a whirl.

Sunlit glass, it twinkles bright,
Reflecting nature's pure delight,
A hedgehog wearing rollerblades,
Zooming by in leafy parades.

Each leaf a comic book so bold,
Tales of laughter to be told,
Crickets chirp in rhyme and jest,
Nature's joke—it's simply the best!

Framed in laughter, hues collide,
Here in fun, we all reside,
With every glance, a chuckle grows,
In this green, the joy just flows.

Framing the Symphony of Spring

Birds compose a cheerful song,
Nature invites us to join along,
A bear on a bike goes by,
Waving with a friendly sigh.

Flowers laugh, they wear a grin,
A jester's hat, where to begin?
Honeybees do the tango there,
As bugs offer up their funny flair.

Wind chimes giggle, lightly sway,
Making music, come what may,
The daisies chuckle, petals twist,
In this frame, who could resist?

In colors bold, the season plays,
Framed in humor, bright sun rays,
Nature's symphony, we adore,
In this joy, we find much more!

A Sightline to Earth's Embrace

A squirrel stole my sandwich, what a sight,
He waved his tail, full of delight.
I laughed as he chomped, crumbs in the breeze,
While birds mocked me, perched high on the trees.

Sunbeams tickle my nose and cheeks,
As I spy on ants plotting sneaky techniques.
They march like soldiers, tiny brigade,
While I sip my lemonade, feeling parade.

A frog jumps by with a comedic plop,
His belly flops down, a circus on hop.
I clap and I cheer, this show of the wild,
Nature's own comedy, forever beguiled.

With every glance, I catch silly scenes,
Like raccoons in hats, living out dreams.
Through glassy frames, life's laughter unfolds,
In moments like these, pure joy never olds.

Eden's Reflection on Transparent Walls

I saw a gnome, garden's prankster bright,
Waving his hat to a passing kite.
The flowers giggled, petals aglow,
At the gnome's silly dance, free with the flow.

Bumblebees buzzing in a jazzy song,
Swaying to rhythms that all feel wrong.
I laughed out loud at their bumbling flight,
A garden soirée, what a joyful sight!

A snail in a race, slow but bold,
Overtaking a stone, or so I'm told.
His tiny triumph, a victory sweet,
In the field of laughter, he can't be beat.

Through sparkling panes, reflections invite,
Silly shenanigans dance in the light.
Nature's own chuckles, caught in my view,
Each moment a gem, a comedic cue.

Leaves Dancing in Silken Sunlight

Leaves whirl like dancers, under the sun,
A breezy tango, just having fun.
They flutter and twirl, an elegant ballet,
Nature's own party, come join the fray!

A chipmunk slipped, on acorn and sprawl,
He scurried and tumbled, oh what a fall!
With a shake of his head and a twitch of his tail,
He gave me a look, as if to exhale.

Sunlight breaks through, to tickle the grass,
While shadows play hide-and-seek as they pass.
The garden's alive, with chuckles galore,
As laughter and sunshine dance on my floor.

A butterfly winks, landing just near,
Her colors flash bright, spreading good cheer.
In this joyful realm, absurdity thrives,
With every bright moment, hilarity dives.

Inside Out: The Garden's Heart

Inside my haven, what a sight indeed,
Daisies wear hats, it's quite the creed.
Worms throw a feast, confetti in mud,
While grasshoppers join in, to dance in the flood.

A curious cat, with a crooked grin,
Chases shadows, it's where fun begins.
He fumbles and tumbles, in the rich soil,
This garden's a stage, for laughter's true toil.

The tomatoes debate, a quirky debate,
Which one's the reddest? They can't seem to wait.
While carrots laugh, and the onions shed tears,
Life's quirky moments, bring joy through the years.

Glass glimmers with stories of the unseen,
As the garden blooms with the absurd and serene.
Each glance reveals, in sun's playful sway,
Humor in nature, in its own funny way.

An Escape Through Colorful Frames

Behind the glass, a world so bright,
A cat's best chance to take a flight.
With a leap and a bound, up to the sill,
She plots her escape, a puppy to thrill.

The flowers wave in a playful cheer,
As butterflies dance, come near, come near!
Each flicker of color brings a grin,
While a grumpy squirrel shouts, 'Get in!'

Oh, the fun of a leaf pile, big and loud!
The view from the frame makes her oh-so-proud.
But a sudden rain turns plans awry,
Back to her perch, she lets out a sigh.

Yet still she dreams of the day ahead,
When the sun shines bright on her dream-filled bed.
With a wink and a stretch, she plots anew,
Her colorful frames will bring her through!

Scurried Secrets of the Outside World

There's a dance of shadows, a fluttering plan,
The floppy-eared rabbit plays fast, than ran.
While the peeking daffodils giggle and sway,
They whisper the secrets of spring and play.

Oh, a rogue wind tousles a curious brain,
As the view unfolds, a quirky refrain.
What's behind that bush? A dashing fox?
Or maybe just trouble, in mismatched socks?

With binocular eyes, the cat takes a scan,
Is that a lost shoe, or just a old can?
The secrets of life scurry by day,
With laughter, she watches, come what may.

The world outside is a comic book page,
Each chapter brings giggles, a laugh-filled stage.
Through her frame so poised, all colors swirl,
The joy of her kingdom, her secret world!

The Garden's Gaze at Daybreak

As morning breaks with a zany grin,
The flowers yawn wide, soft petals spin.
A bee in a bowtie buzzes on through,
With nectar-doused dreams and a dance long overdue.

The sun stretches tall with a giggling ray,
Chasing sleepy bugs as they stretch for the day.
A ladybug waddles, quite proud of her spots,
While the daisies gossip, sharing their thoughts.

The garden erupts in a raucous cheer,
While the snoring old gnome simply won't clear.
Ghosts of the night drift away in delight,
As the blossoms burst open, ready for flight.

Oh, what a spectacle, the day has begun!
With laughter and whispers, oh what fun!
The garden abounds with colors so bright,
As it greets the new day, a whimsical sight!

Flower-Laden Breaths from Afar

Scented breezes waltz by with flair,
Taking the cat by surprise in her chair.
Each whiff tells tales of a world unseen,
Where butterflies prance, all colors so keen.

"Is that a pizza smell?" she giggles in jest,
"Or just the sunflowers having a fest?"
With blossoms so wild, she jigs on the floor,
Imagining feasts from her bright window door.

And then out pops a snail, oh so slow,
Munching leaves like it's a fine gourmet show.
While the ants parade, a spaghetti-like line,
Each carrying dreams made of twine and sunshine.

She dreams of a picnic, the best kind of fun,
With flower-laden breezes under the sun.
Outside her frame, the adventure is grand,
Filled with laughter and whimsy, all carefully planned!

Glances of Flora and Mirage

In the garden, blooms collide,
Petals racing side by side.
Beetles sporting shades of gold,
Telling tales too wild and bold.

Breezes tickle daisies tall,
As butterflies begin to sprawl.
With a splash of color spree,
Who knew plants could dance with glee?

Imagine flowers with a flair,
They gossip in the sunny air.
With winks and nods, they tease and play,
Inviting all to join the fray.

So, next time you wander near,
Pause and lend a listening ear.
For nature's laughter rings so true,
In glances shared by me and you.

Enchanted Landscapes at Dawn

As sunbeams stretch their lazy arms,
The garden wakes with playful charms.
A rooster crows in silly tune,
While goats prance round, a comic boon.

Deer don pajamas as they graze,
Caught snoozing in the morning haze.
A squirrel slips on dew-kissed grass,
Laughter echoes as it falls with sass.

Caterpillars race for the prize,
With leaf-shaped caps and cheeky eyes.
Each blossom chuckles in its shade,
Stories of silly escapades.

So when you rise and greet the sun,
Remember, nature loves to run.
In every bloom and every sound,
Funny tales of joy abound.

Rustling Leaves in Hidden Frames

Leaves giggle with the slightest breeze,
Tickling branches like a tease.
In their rustle, secrets bloom,
Whispers shared beyond the gloom.

Old owls wear glasses, they confide,
Observing antics from their hide.
With wise old grins, they nod with glee,
At follies of their leafy spree.

A chipmunk juggles acorns round,
While tree trunks give a booming sound.
Nature's parlor, filled with jest,
In this realm, the uproar's best.

So stroll among the rustling shades,
Watch the wonders that evades.
For laughter dwells in every leaf,
A garden of joy beyond belief.

Raindrops Dancing on Green Glades

Pitter-patter, a joyful sound,
Raindrops leap from ground to ground.
Frogs don tap shoes to the beat,
Creating rhythms, oh so sweet!

Clouds don mustaches, oh so grand,
As flowers sway in raindrop bands.
Each drop whispers a silly tale,
Of splashes made in nature's sail.

Silly ants in raincoats hurry,
While worms squirm in gleeful flurry.
Every puddle's a laughing face,
Inviting all to join the race.

So dance along, let worries flee,
In a world of raindrop glee.
For laughter flows like streams so bright,
In nature's show, pure delight.

Green Shadows and Playful Light

In a garden where squirrels plot,
A cabbage conspires with a pot.
Leaves giggle in the sunny gleam,
Nature's laughter, a leafy dream.

Bouncing shadows, they try to hide,
While sneaky ants take a joyride.
Sunbeams tickle the grass so bright,
Making everything feel just right.

Colors dance in a carefree whirl,
Butterflies twirling, giving a twirl.
Flowers blush with a playful sigh,
While dandelions wave goodbye.

A snail trips over an acorn's cap,
In this world, it's all a jolly slap.
As giggles echo through the soft air,
Nature's joke, just beyond compare.

The Dance of Leaves in Gentle Winds

Leaves whisper secrets, not so discreet,
They chuckle as they lose their seat.
A breeze mumbles, 'Hold on tight!'
But they flutter down, what a silly sight!

Squirrels frolic, with acorns in tow,
Do they know where they're meant to go?
Each leap and bound, a comical show,
Under the sun's warm, golden glow.

A chubby crow breaks into song,
With notes that waver, nothing wrong!
The trees sway in delightful glee,
As laughter blends with harmony.

All is merry, in this leafy domain,
Where whimsy and fun are bound to reign.
With every rustle, a giggle is found,
In this playful dance, joy knows no bound.

A Treetop Tale Through Crystal Glass

Peering through a quirky pane,
A curious cat is going insane.
Birds giggle from the nearby tree,
Singing tunes, just to tease me!

A raccoon dons a monocle proud,
Declaring himself the king of the crowd.
He waggles his tail with snobbish flair,
While mockingbirds join in the jest with care.

To the left, the sun makes a splash,
Reflecting off puddles, it's pure panache!
A funny frog leaps into the glaze,
Creating ripples in a laugh-filled daze.

The laughter echoes, a whimsical sound,
As whispers of humor swirl all around.
Through glassy heights, each joke takes flight,
A tree-bound comedy, what sheer delight!

Play of Shadow on Leafy Canvas

Under the boughs where shadows race,
A cheeky squirrel finds his place.
With acorns flying, an aerial show,
Painting the ground with a comical glow.

The sun peeks through, a nosy friend,
While shadows play, on them depend.
A dance of light in a game so grand,
Where giggles erupt from the dry, warm land.

Caterpillars wear tiny hats,
As munching leaves say, 'What of that?'
They shuffle along, in a slow parade,
Confetti of crumbs, their grand charade.

Laughing lilies sway with flair,
In the garden's gossip, all is fair.
As shadows blend on this canvas bright,
The merriment grows in the soft dusk light.

The Odyssey Beyond the Glass

As I gaze through this glass, oh what a sight,
A chicken wearing glasses, such a silly delight.
The cat in a bow tie, elegant and spry,
And a squirrel with a top hat, waving bye-bye.

A dog on a skateboard, zooming past trees,
While ants throw a party, dancing with ease.
I chuckle and laugh, what a peculiar crew,
In this canvas of chaos, life feels brand new.

A fish with a mustache swims up to the pane,
While a rabbit in socks jumps around with great gain.
With every odd moment, joy fills the air,
Behind this clear barrier, laughter's laid bare.

As the sun starts to set, it paints quite the scene,
A parade of mischief wrapped up in bright green.
Through this portal of whimsy, I'm endlessly blessed,
For the oddities here surely outshine the rest.

Envisioning Eden's Delight

Peering through my portal, oh what a display,
A llama in pajamas, frolicking in play.
With fruit hats and giggles, they jive to the tune,
Who knew paradise came with such laughter at noon?

A garden of veggies, all taking a stroll,
An onion in a bowler, feeling quite whole.
Each carrot is chatting, with peas in a pod,
In this Eden of nonsense, my heart's all agog.

There's a radish in slippers, with dreams on its mind,
And a cabbage in heels, oh so hard to find.
In this wild, silly garden, I chuckle and sigh,
What a marvelous world just beyond this glass eye.

With sunlight and laughter, the day drifts away,
I smile at the whimsy that colors my stay.
Through the laughter and chaos, life's vivid embrace,
With each glance outside, joy finds its own place.

Clusters of Joy through Soft Openings

Through the opening soft, what a quirky delight,
A porcupine dancing in shiny moonlight.
With twirls and with spins, it pricks in the air,
Inviting all critters for a whimsical share.

A pineapple sunglasses-wearing bird on the fly,
Sings ballads to daisies as they wave goodbye.
The flowers are giggling, as bees wear their hats,
In this gathering of joy, there's no time for spats.

Bunnies on pogo sticks bounce with such glee,
While owls tap their watches, sipping tea by the tree.
Each glance through this opening is a brand new charm,
Where silliness blossoms and stirs up no harm.

As laughter spills out, like bubbles in spring,
Every creature's invited to join in and sing.
So here's to the joy, through each heartfelt peek,
Life's funny parade brings smiles to the meek.

Reflections on Nature's Vivid Tapestry

Through this view so bright, a tapestry gleams,
With frogs in bow ties and whimsical dreams.
They croak out a tune, as butterflies twirl,
In nature's wild dance, watch the colors unfurl.

A turtle on roller skates zips past the frame,
While a goldfish in bubbles is claiming its fame.
Each ripple of laughter flows freely and bold,
In this vibrant reflection, a story unfolds.

With unicorns prancing, their manes all aglow,
And squirrels with their glasses, putting on a show.
Every creature's a star in this comical play,
Where nature's bright canvas invites us to stay.

So peek through this portal, where fun has a flair,
In the kaleidoscope world, joy dances in air.
With each lively glance, let happiness weave,
The reflections so bright, they're hard to believe.

Lush Life Outside the Glass

Squirrels in top hats dance around,
Chasing each other, laughter abound.
A pigeon gives the royal wave,
While ants march like they're on a rave.

Sunshine spills a golden treat,
Flowers pirouette in the heat.
A cat peers out, all serious face,
Wonders why there's no dinner race.

Emerald Hues in Morning Light

Leaves whisper secrets, green and spry,
A leaf just sneezed—oh my, oh my!
Morning dew giggles on the ground,
As sunlight twirls, joy all around.

Bees don top hats, buzzing to work,
Waltzing with daisies, oh what a quirk!
A snail in shades, slow but grand,
Takes the high road, not as planned.

Framed Fronds and Whispering Winds

Fronds flutter like a cheeky flag,
As breezes tell secrets, then quite lag.
A robin sits, plays a tune so sweet,
While dancing shadows swap their feet.

Tickled by air, a clumsy bee,
Bumps a daffodil saying, "Excuse me!"
Then flowers giggle, a blossomed crowd,
"Oh look, the bee's got lost! How loud!"

Glistening Drops on Leafy Embrace

Raindrops play hopscotch on green blades,
Each splash a laugh, in nature's parades.
Caterpillars wear tiny raincoats,
While crickets try to sing like boats.

A snail surfs down a slick, wet road,
Finding the joy in his sticky load.
With splashes and giggles in the air,
It's a soggy party; come, if you dare!

Imagined Wilderness at Arm's Length

In my room, shadows play,
A giraffe in pajamas might sway.
Cacti wear hats that look quite absurd,
While squirrels dance, chattering unheard.

Nature's cranky neighbor, a toucan loud,
Yells at my plants, forming a crowd.
The fridge hums tunes of a distant stream,
As I sip my tea, lost in a dream.

Rivulets of Life Through a Clear Lens

Raindrops tap-dance on my sill,
Squirrels hold meetings, plotting their thrill.
The curtains tease with a gentle sway,
While ants host a picnic, a grand buffet.

Outside the storm, a squirrel debates,
To steal my snacks or negotiate states?
Laughter echoes through the soft rain,
As I watch the world shrug off its disdain.

A Threshold for Verdant Vistas

My garden's a circus of leafy delight,
Worms in top hats twirl round, oh what a sight!
With daisies as ushers, they greet the snails,
While chipmunks stage plays, telling tall tales.

Vines throw parties, tangling in glee,
While daisies sing hymns to the bumblebee.
The barbecue smokes up dreamy delight,
As shadows of critters dance in the night.

Where Joy and Nature Converge

In the garden, a breeze tickles my chin,
While a gnome snores loudly, content in his win.
The sun pulls faces, teasing the clouds,
As flowers gossip, forming their crowds.

Butterflies wearing capes flutter about,
While grasshoppers rhyme, singing out loud.
Nature's a jester, laughing with me,
As I cherish these quirks, so wild and free.

Windowsill Dreams of Abundance

A pot of herbs, a gardener's fate,
Basil's winks, oh how they mate!
Tomatoes hide in shy retreat,
Planning a heist of summer's treat.

The sunbeam dances, the dust takes flight,
A ladybug says, 'I'm here for a bite!'
Bees form a band, all set to groove,
In this wild quest, we all improve.

Lettuce giggles as it grows so tall,
Gossipy peas hear the fruits recall,
A radish whispers, 'Look at me shine!'
They're all convinced they're divine!

From windowsill dreams, the cheer we pluck,
A salad party, oh what luck!
With every sprout, our joy increases,
Nature's joke? Life never ceases!

Captured Green: A Botanical View

A fern in shoes, what a sight to behold,
Claiming the corner, feeling quite bold!
In a world of dirt, it wears a crown,
Dancing in sunlight, never a frown.

Succulents giggle, in pots they conspire,
Counting the water, their secret desire.
Cactus makes faces, prickly yet fun,
'Can't touch this,' it shouts, 'I'm number one!'

Vines creep up like they're training for fame,
Whispering secrets, they play a wild game.
Basil does yoga, stretching his leaves,
'Breathe deep,' he instructs, as nature believes.

Behind closed curtains, the antics ignite,
A festival of green, all day and night.
Laughing at sunlight, playing with shades,
Captured green dreams in wild cascades.

The Fragrance of Lush Perspectives.

In a sunny nook, the herbs have a chat,
Rosemary brags, 'I'm good in a spat!'
Mint jumps around, all fresh and spry,
'Mix me with laughter,' she flutters nearby.

Chives try to whisper, however, they squeak,
'Don't underestimate, I'm never weak!'
Thyme rolls its eyes, 'I'm pungent, you see,
Add me to dishes, I'm the VIP!'

Petunias laugh, petals painted bright,
'We'll outshine the sun, that's our delight!'
Lilies do pirouettes, putting on shows,
'Join us in blooming, that's how it goes!'

With humor in hues, they rise and they twirl,
In the jolly garden, a fragrant whirl.
The air filled with giggles, a fragrant dance,
In this chase for joy, life gives us a chance!

Soft Glimpses of Green

A window opens, greens peek through,
'Is that sunlight?' they cheer, how true!
Creeping ivy throws a party today,
With leaves in a frenzy, they twist and sway.

Potted pals, in a wild embrace,
'We're in this together, let's win this race!'
A sleepy sunflower yawns with grace,
As daisies perform a soft, rhythmic chase.

A squirrel strolls in, wearing a grin,
Scavenging greens, he thinks it's a win!
New thyme sprigs point, 'Look at our guest!'
In this jumbled space, they feel truly blessed.

With soft glimpses of all things bright,
A window of humor, pure delight.
In the laughter of leaves, life twists and turns,
In every green tale, a lesson it earns!

Enraptured by Verdant Beauty

In a garden of leaves, I found a frog,
He croaked a tune, I laughed like a dog.
With flowers in hats, they danced all day,
While sunbeams giggled in a playful way.

The daisies wore shades, the roses played pretend,
A bee in a tux, trying to mend.
Butterflies spun in a dizzying flight,
Chasing their dreams, oh what a sight!

A worm told jokes, he's the life of the pot,
Each laugh a ripple, each chuckle, a lot.
In nature's own theatre, the cast was quite bold,
With stories of laughter, they boldly told.

So join in the fun, let your spirits sway,
With a wink from the leaves, chase the blues away.
For in this green world, we find our way back,
To joy's little moments, a colorful track.

The Horizon Beyond the Frames

Staring through glass, the scene is a hoot,
A squirrel in a tie, how very astute!
He jumps with a flair, a nut in his mouth,
Singing sweet songs of his treasure from south.

The clouds wear crowns, they float by so free,
While raindrops tap-dance, what a sight to see!
A cat in a bowler, quite proud of his strut,
Looks out at the world from his cozy little rut.

Chasing the sun is a misfit crew,
A turtle in shades, a snail slipping through.
They plot grand adventures, much to their delight,
Making each moment a whimsical flight.

Outside the frames, life does abound,
With giggles and grins that dance all around.
So lift up your gaze, to the horizon so bright,
Where laughter and mischief fill each day and night.

Serenade of Butterflies in Bloom

In a patch of bright blooms, a party was set,
With butterflies twirling, I'd place my bet.
Their colors like rainbows, a whimsical team,
They danced with the daisies, oh what a dream!

In a petal-brewed punch, drunk on delight,
A ladybug waltzed, twinkling at night.
The ants played the drums, a beat to adore,
While crickets hummed tunes, and flew out the door.

Each blossom was laughing, in sun's golden gaze,
With petals that shimmered, in nature's own craze.
A bumblebee DJ spun vintage tunes,
As everyone grooved under radiant moons.

"Oh, join us," they beckon, "don't be such a bore,
Just sway on the breeze, and let laughter soar!"
In this carnival of life, so silly, so bold,
We celebrate colors, as stories unfold.

Soft Echoes from Leafy Vale

A woodpecker's knock, a drummer at play,
In leafy vale echoes, they shout hooray!
With trunks in their tuxes, the trees laugh and sway,
While shadows join in for a sunlit ballet.

Down by the brook, frogs throw a soirée,
While turtles join in with a slow, easy sway.
A fish slips a wink, as he charts his fate,
In giggles and splashes, oh what a great date!

The breeze tells a secret of frolic and fun,
"Let's race to the hills, before day is done!"
With a rustle of laughter, they gather around,
In whispers of joy, life's magic is found.

So gather your friends, let the mirth come alive,
In nature's embrace, where the giggles thrive.
For every sound, every rustle, each cheer,
Is a reminder that joy is always near.

Illusions of Calm Through Glassy Eyes

Looking out, I spy a cat,
Prowling past, where ducks are fat.
A squirrel steals a sandwich crust,
While I sip tea, it's a must.

The mailman trips, his shoelace torn,
I chuckle, having a fine morn.
A bird with sass steals my biscuit,
Nature's show, oh so brisket!

Raindrops dance on my pane of glass,
Like tiny tap dancers, they pass.
I giggle as they bubble down,
A liquid race in this sleepy town.

With every glance, new antics unfold,
A world so silly, never gets old.
From my perch, I watch the fun,
Through glassy eyes, I feel like one.

A Portal to Eden's Embrace

Bees buzzing in a wild parade,
They're up to mischief, unafraid.
While flowers gossip, colors collude,
The petals laugh, it's quite a mood.

A gopher pops up, then vanishes fast,
Like a magician, his trick unsurpassed.
I pray he doesn't take my shoe,
That little rascal, he's got a view!

Pigeons strut in their finest attire,
With beaks a-chatter, they never tire.
I hear them claim the best parking spot,
Oh those feathered pals, I love the plot.

A portal here, with laughter and cheer,
Eden's embrace, it's crystal clear.
Through the glass, a vivid delight,
Where fun and mischief take flight.

Serenades from the Outside World

An opera sung by the noisy crows,
With flair and talent, they strike a pose.
Their raucous tunes fill the morning air,
I can't help but giggle, it's only fair.

The dogs below plot a grand escape,
With wagging tails, forming a shape.
They bark for treats, their clever ruse,
This live concert, I simply can't refuse.

A lawn mower sings a tiresome song,
While neighbors' karaoke screams along.
I chuckle as I sip my brew,
The outside world, a lively zoo.

In a symphony of laughs and barks,
These serenades light up the parks.
Through this portal, life's playful sound,
In my glass framed view, joy is found.

Melodies from Blooming Vistas

Daisies sway like they run a band,
Their petals dance, it's truly grand.
A butterfly flits, dressed in style,
Painting smiles, all the while.

The breeze whispers jokes to the trees,
While clouds play tag, oh what a tease!
I chuckle as they tumble and spin,
In nature's theater, let the fun begin.

A gardener spills her seeds with glee,
As birds rush in for an impromptu spree.
With beaks that giggle, they dive and swoop,
Amidst the flowers, they form a troop.

Each bloom a tale, each laugh a cheer,
In blooming vistas, joy draws near.
Through the glass, I soak in the play,
Melodies brightening my day.

The Color of Enchantment Beyond

In the garden, gnomes are grinning,
With colors bright, they're all spinning.
Flowers whisper jokes, you see,
Bees buzz along, oh so carefree.

Bunnies hop with tiny hats,
While dancing cats chase after rats.
Sunlight spills like lemonade,
Each moment's a circus parade.

Clouds float by like thoughts in flight,
Scarecrows laugh till it's twilight.
Even rainbows tell their tales,
Of silly winds and playful gales.

So peek beyond the vine and leaf,
Find hidden smiles, and never grieve.
Life's a riot, take a glance,
At nature's wild and wacky dance.

Peering Into Nature's Canvas

Squirrels paint with acorn ink,
They giggle when they stop to think.
With each brush in fluffy paws,
They sketch the world without a pause.

Butterflies wear shoes of lace,
And waltz around with nerdy grace.
Mice play chess on toadstool tops,
While dandelions flip and flop.

The breeze carries a melody,
Of trees that dance so merrily.
Lively colors splash and gleam,
In this funny nature dream.

So wave to every critter there,
With polka dots and crazy hair.
Art thrives where we least expect,
Nature's whimsy—oh, perfect!

A Glimpse of Eden's Splendor

Chickens cluck in a rapping band,
Playing tunes with flapping hands.
A rooster steals the limelight bright,
As sunflowers sway, laughing outright.

In this patch of pure delight,
Veggies challenge views on height.
Radishes wear capes, so bold,
Whispering tales from days of old.

Feathery friends team up for fun,
While carrots race to hug the sun.
Nature's best comedians here,
Spreading laughs and a bit of cheer.

So let's giggle, dance, and play,
In this verdant cabaret.
Life's a show, just look around,
In laughter's grip, we're tightly bound.

Leafy Echoes of Stillness

Trees gossip in rustling tones,
Sharing stories of their bones.
Leaves chuckle, tickled by the breeze,
Swinging gently with such ease.

A crow croaks jokes that thrill,
As puddles collect laughter still.
Fungi fashion quirky hats,
Inviting toads to socialize with bats.

Moss sits back, enjoying the show,
While shadows dance and gently glow.
In this calm, the world can tease,
With nature's humor sure to please.

So pause to hear the verdant jest,
Enjoy the quirks—it's truly best.
In echoes soft, the giggles blend,
Nature's charm, our best friend.

Revelations of a Private Eden

Behind the glass, a jungle plays,
Where squirrels debate on sunny days.
The flowers gossip in whispering tones,
As bees hum melodies, not in drones.

A cat on the sill, with a skeptical eye,
Judges the antics of birds that fly.
While a rose tries to catch every laugh,
But blooms are shy, hiding their craft.

The sun's shining jokes light up the scene,
As ivy climbs with a mischievous sheen.
Plants throw a party, dressed in their best,
While gnomes compete in a garden quest.

Laughter erupts from the daisies bright,
Who tickle the grass with pure delight.
Nature's whimsy sprinkles joy like confetti,
In this paradise where all is heady.

Dreams Woven in Greenery

In a tapestry woven with vibrant hues,
The petals share secrets and playful views.
A hedgehog prances, stepping with flair,
While the daisies chuckle, lacking a care.

Sunlight bounces off leaves like a joke,
As critters gather, and laughter invokes.
The wind whispers tales of the day ahead,
While mushrooms toast to the fun they spread.

A mischievous squirrel, with acorn in paw,
Nods at the daisies, impressively raw.
Behind closed curtains, the world spins around,
While the houseplants plot mischief, unbound.

Each branch and bud, a story to share,
With giggles and guffaws filling the air.
In this merry haven, all worries are few,
As nature unfolds her delightful view.

An Oasis of Sights Beyond

Through a shimmer of leaves, the stories unfold,
As animals gather, both brave and bold.
The ferns crack jokes, while lilies conspire,
In a world of green where laughter won't tire.

A butterfly flutters with charm and grace,
Teasing a snail in a slow-motion race.
While crickets chirp in a humorous chant,
Mimicking birds with a favorite rant.

Sunshine spills into every nook and cranny,
As flowers wag tails, a sight that's uncanny.
The breeze is a jester with tickling hands,
Whisking away worries, just like grains of sands.

Each scene transforms in a playful twist,
As nature's comedians play on the list.
From petals to pranks, let the laughter ignite,
In this vibrant space, everything feels right.

Sunbeams Dancing on Flourishing Fields

In fields where sunbeams play hide and seek,
The daisies giggle, their laughter unique.
A bumblebee winks, full of sweet charm,
As tulips tease him, with bright colors arm.

The grass bows low in a comedic sway,
While ladybugs join in the playful fray.
Clouds drift by with a whimsical view,
As shadows dance in a lively tableau.

A rabbit hops over, all fluffy and spry,
And challenges sunbeams to a game in the sky.
With each joyful bounce, a ripple of cheer,
Turns the calm meadows into laughter's frontier.

In harmony sung, under azure skies,
Nature's own stand-up where everyone tries.
So come take a peek, don't worry or fret,
In this joyous domain, there's always a set.

Kaleidoscope of Lush Imagery

Colors dance, a vibrant spree,
Greens and reds, wild jubilee.
Leaves gossip with the cheerful breeze,
While flowers giggle, buzzing with bees.

Chirping birds in silly flight,
Twirl around in pure delight.
A butterfly with fancy flair,
Winks at me, oh what a pair!

Sunlight flickers, shadows play,
Tickling petals that sway and sway.
A mushroom dude, with polka dots,
Grins at us from his cozy spot.

Nature's palette, bold and bright,
Creates a scene, a comical sight.
With every glance, new humor shows,
In this garden where laughter grows.

Breezes That Kiss the Open Spaces

Winds blow kisses on sunlit cheeks,
Rustling through the grass that creaks.
A silly squirrel drops his snack,
Chasing it down, oh what a whack!

Dandelion fluff in merry flight,
Sailing off, oh what a sight!
Kids in awe, they start to chase,
As giggles fill the open space.

A kite gets stuck in a tree's embrace,
Bobbing gently, in a funny race.
The sky so blue, the sun so bright,
Everyone's grinning, what pure delight!

With breezes that play, so carefree,
Nature's humor brings us glee.
Through whispering leaves that tease and play,
Life dances joyfully, every day.

Visions of Growth in Stillness

Roots stretch deep, like legs on a couch,
Finding comfort in the earth's slouch.
While daisies wink with their bright white hats,
Telling jokes to nearby chitchat.

A worm spins tales, quite absurd,
In muddy realms, he's the wordy bird.
He wriggles, giggles, full of charm,
Spreading laughter with his squirmy warm.

Time pauses here, it seems to play,
As flowers grin in a soft ballet.
They sway and bow, take gentle turns,
While nature's humor brightly burns.

Through each still moment, joy appears,
A tapestry woven with laughter and cheers.
In a garden where humor sprouts,
Life grows sillier, without a doubt.

Nature's Whispers Through Transparent Barriers

Through glassy panes, the world unfolds,
A parade of colors, stories told.
Silly frogs leap, their tongues outstretched,
Catching flies—they seem so wretched!

Leaves chatter softly, secrets shared,
Tickling thoughts, as funny as dared.
The wind plays tricks with shadows near,
Swooshing giggles that we can hear.

Petunias pose as models bright,
Strutting petals in sheer delight.
A spider spins in wobbly grace,
Creating art in the silliest place.

Through barriers clear, life winks and quips,
Nature's humor dances, never slips.
In this world where laughter grows,
Joy bursts forth, and everyone knows.

Beyond the Pane of Serenity

In a world where dust bunnies play,
My neighbors think I've gone astray.
They sip their tea with dignified grace,
While I'm stuck in this hilarious space.

Birds tap-dance on the glass with glee,
They peek at me, and I giggle with spree.
A cat outside gives me a stare,
I wave back—oh, how life seems fair!

The Lush Canvas from Within

Painting the day with laughter so bright,
I spill my coffee—oh, what a sight!
The flowers sing songs of pastel delight,
While I juggle fruit—what a silly plight!

Sunshine bounces, a game in the air,
I'm tickled pink by the cheeky glare.
Outside, the squirrels race with pure delight,
They've stolen my snacks, those furry blight!

Fragrant Views of Timeless Growth

The flowers gossip through the glass,
While I slip and fall—oh, what class!
Nature chuckles at my clumsy declare,
As bees buzz by in perfect flair.

The herbs on my sill plot a prank,
Every time I water, they tank.
With each sunny day, my laughter grows,
In this botanical show, who knows how it flows!

Hues of Life Beyond the Barrier

Colors outside are a vibrant joke,
A rainbow appears—it's not just smoke!
The grass waves 'hello,' what a sight it seems,
While I dance with shadows, lost in dreams.

A tree wearing socks knocks at my door,
Inviting me out for some silliness galore.
I chuckle and clap at this oddity keen,
Life's truly hilariously serene!

Fragments of Nature's Canvas

A squirrel in a bow tie, nut in paw,
Flashing peeks like a furry little law.
Leaves rustle secrets of a dancing bee,
Spreading mischief from branch to tree.

A bird in a fedora sings off key,
Chasing raindrops like wild confetti.
Flowers giggle in hues of bright laughs,
Nature's art forms whimsical graphs.

Caterpillars host a tea party grand,
Wobbling guests with a wobbly hand.
Grass blades hum melodies soft and slight,
Each wiggle creating laughter in flight.

Oh, how the bugs join the jolly fun,
Dressed in outfits out of the sun!
Frogs jump in to a boisterous tune,
Under the smile of a curious moon.